I0756097

THIS BOOK BELONGS TO:

WELCOME
TO IDAHO
GREAT SEAL OF THE STATE OF IDAHO
ESTO PERPETUA
STATE OF IDAHO

Dedicated to all the explorers.

ISBN 978-1-958985-94-6

www.joeysavestheday.com

Mimi Books™ Publishing

A Mimi Book

Idaho got its name from a word that was once said to mean "gem of the mountains." For many years, people believed it came from a Native American language. Later, historians discovered that the word was actually created by a man named George Willing. Even though the meaning wasn't real, people liked how the name sounded, and Idaho eventually became the official name of the state we know today.

Idaho has a long history that begins with Native American nations who lived among its mountains, rivers, and plains for thousands of years. Groups such as the Shoshone, Nez Perce, and Coeur d'Alene built strong communities across the region. In the early 1800s, explorers, fur traders, and later settlers began arriving. Gold discoveries brought even more people, and new towns slowly grew.

Idaho was the forty-third state to join the Union. It officially joined on July 3, 1890.

43rd

Idaho is located in the northwestern United States. It is bordered by Washington, Oregon, Nevada, Utah, Montana, and Wyoming. To the north, it meets the Canadian province of British Columbia.

Boise is the capital of Idaho.
It officially became the capital in 1864.

Boise, Idaho, has an estimated population of about 238,900 people.
Idaho

There are approximately 1,930,000 people residing in the state of Idaho.

Idaho Falls, Idaho

Idaho is the fourteenth largest
state in the United States by area.
14th
Boise, Idaho

Sacagawea was a young Shoshone woman who played a very important role in American history. She was born in the area that is now Idaho, near the Lemhi River. When she was still a teenager, she helped guide the Lewis and Clark Expedition as they explored the West. Sacagawea knew the land, the plants, and the mountain passes, and she helped the explorers find safe paths. Her bravery, knowledge, and calm spirit made her one of the most admired figures in Idaho's history.

Idaho is famous for its delicious potatoes, grown in the state's rich, volcanic soil. These potatoes are known for being fluffy, flavorful, and perfect for baking, mashing, or turning into crispy fries. Families all across Idaho enjoy them at dinner tables, celebrations, and community events, making potatoes one of the state's most beloved and iconic foods.

IDAHO

There are 44 counties in Idaho.

Here is a list of twenty of those counties:

Bear Lake	Elmore	Latah	Shoshone
Benewah	Franklin	Lemhi	Teton
Bingham	Fremont	Lewis	Twin Falls
Blaine	Gem	Lincoln	Valley
Boise	Gooding	Madison	Washington

Shoshone Falls is one of Idaho's most amazing landmarks and is often called the "Niagara of the West." The waterfall drops 212 feet. It is taller than Niagara Falls and creates a huge curtain of rushing water. In spring, melting snow makes the falls extra powerful, and families can watch the Snake River splash and sparkle as it tumbles over the cliffs.

The first major gold discovery in Idaho didn't happen in a big city; it took place in a quiet mountain valley near what is now Pierce, Idaho. In 1860, a man named Elias D. Pierce and his group of prospectors found gold in the Clearwater River region. This discovery sparked Idaho's very first gold rush, bringing thousands of people into the territory almost overnight. Small camps quickly grew into busy mining towns, and this moment helped shape Idaho's early history.

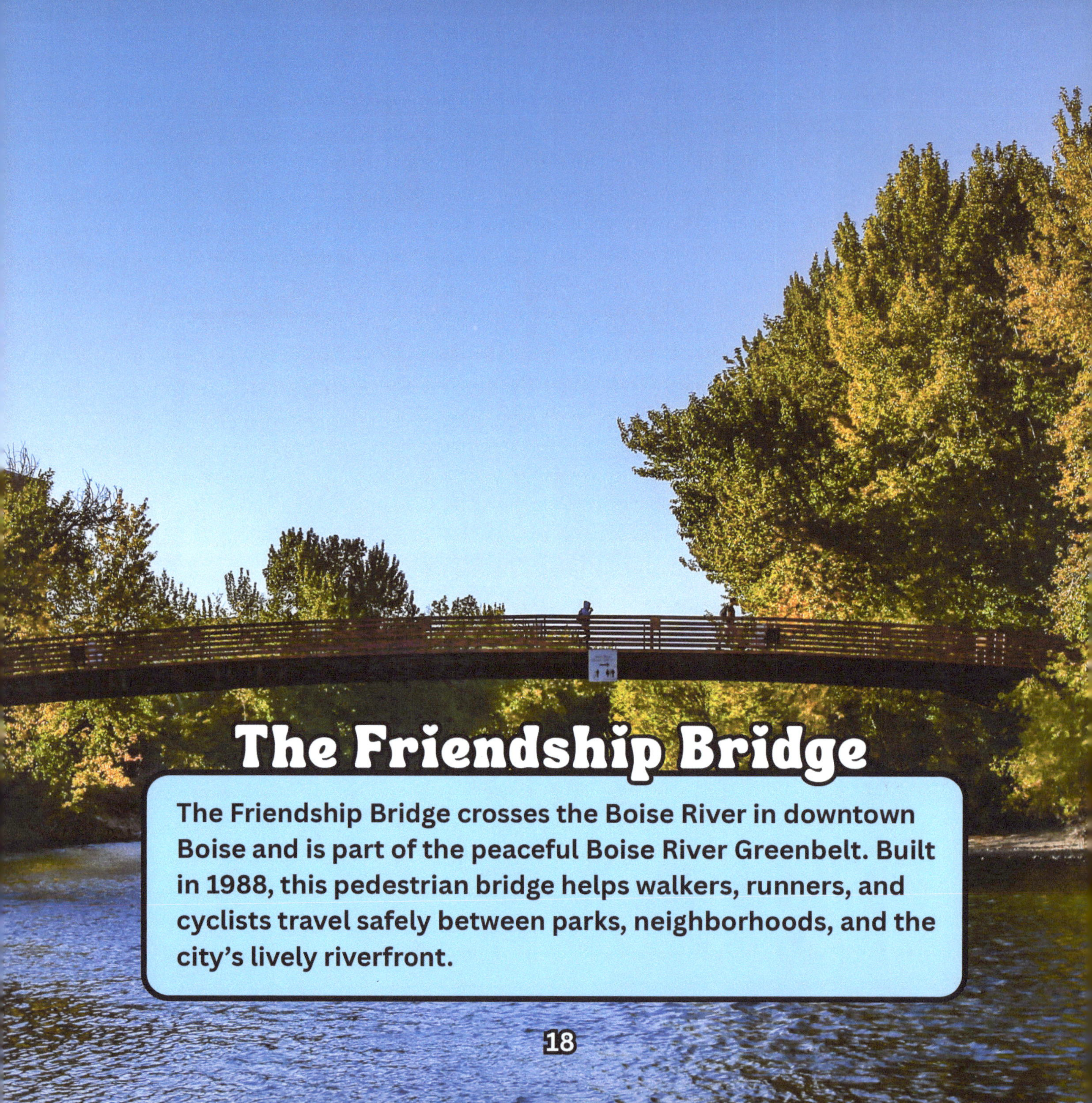

The Friendship Bridge

The Friendship Bridge crosses the Boise River in downtown Boise and is part of the peaceful Boise River Greenbelt. Built in 1988, this pedestrian bridge helps walkers, runners, and cyclists travel safely between parks, neighborhoods, and the city's lively riverfront.

The Idaho state bird is the Mountain Bluebird.
It became the official state bird in 1931.

The official state flower of Idaho is the Syringa. It was chosen as the state flower in 1931.

A couple of Idaho's nicknames include the Gem State and the Potato State.

Idaho's motto is "Esto Perpetua," which is Latin for "Let it be perpetual" or "Let it last forever."

What the motto means:

Idaho hopes its natural beauty, land, and way of life will last forever.

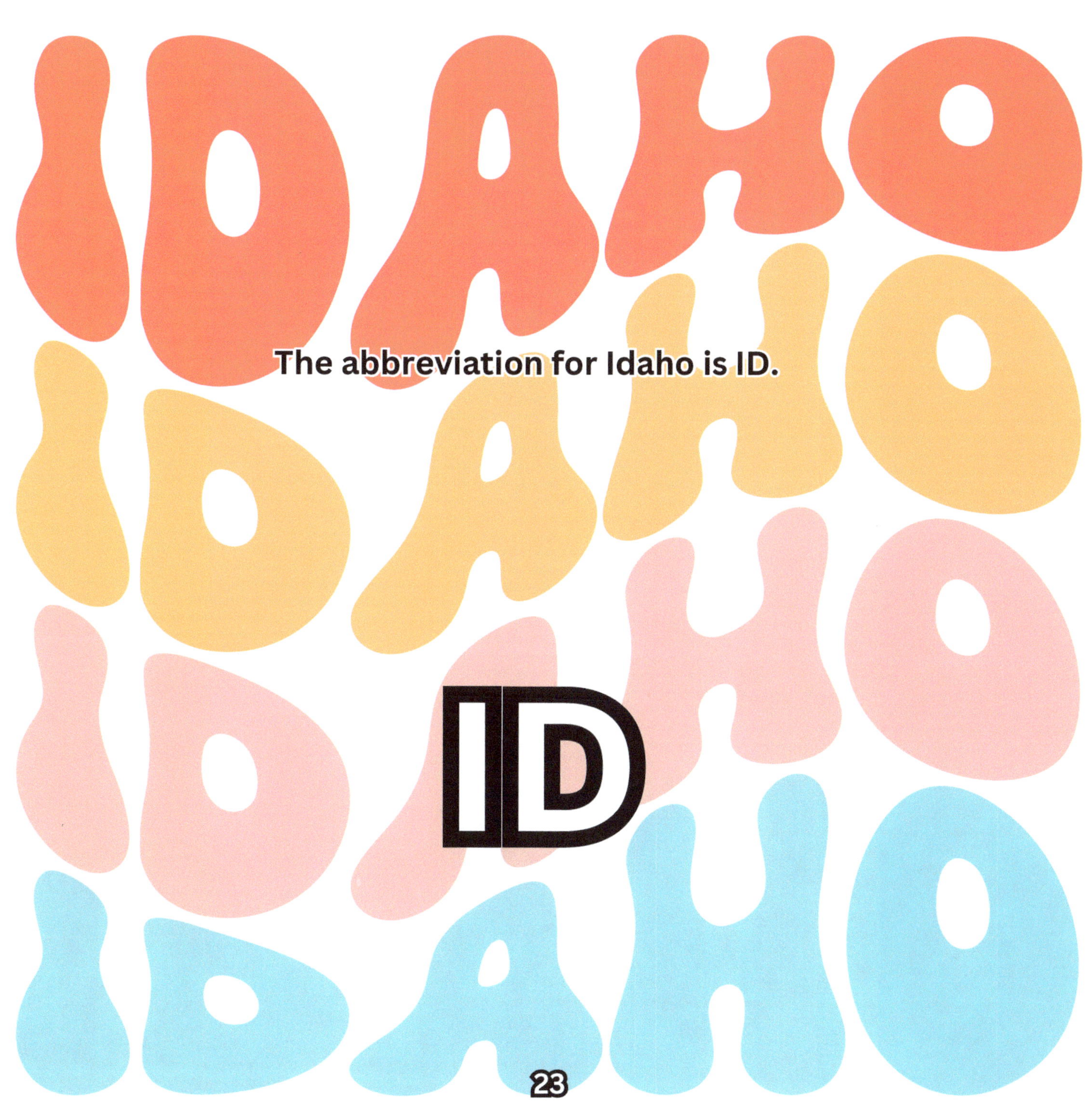

The abbreviation for Idaho is ID.

ID

Idaho's state flag was officially adopted in 1907.

Some crops grown in Idaho are potatoes, wheat, barley, and sugar beets.

Some animals that live in Idaho are elk, moose, black bears, mountain lions, and bald eagles.

Idaho experiences a wide range of temperatures throughout the year. The hottest temperature ever recorded in the state was 118 degrees Fahrenheit, measured in Orofino on July 28, 1934. In contrast, the coldest temperature documented was −60 degrees Fahrenheit, recorded at Island Park Dam on January 18, 1943.

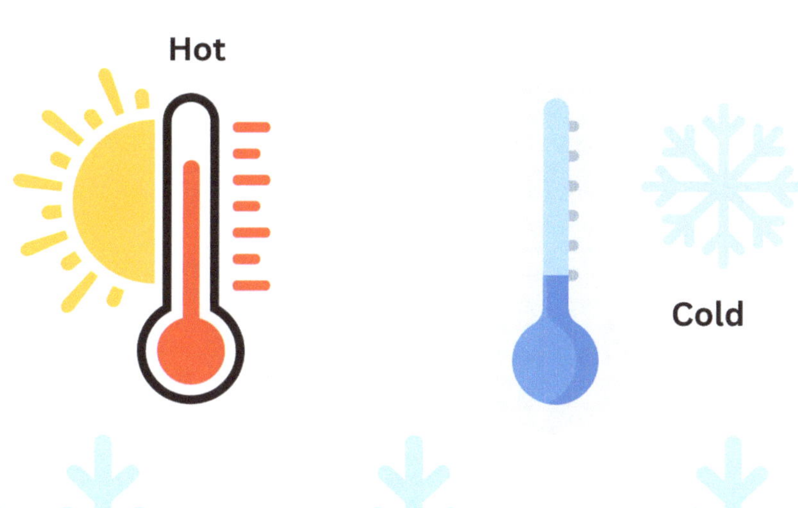

Zoo Idaho in Pocatello is a wonderful place to explore, with animals from many different habitats. Kids can see black bears, bison, mountain lions, otters, and playful monkeys, along with colorful birds and reptiles.

The Cataldo Mission, also called the Mission of the Sacred Heart, is the oldest standing building in Idaho. It was built in the 1850s by Jesuit missionaries and members of the Coeur d'Alene Tribe. Today, it's a historic site where visitors can learn about Idaho's early days.

The largest airport in Idaho is the Boise Airport, located in Boise, the state's capital city. It sits at 3201 West Airport Way and serves as the main travel hub for people flying in and out of Idaho. This airport connects travelers to cities across the country and helps people reach Idaho's mountains, parks, and outdoor adventures.

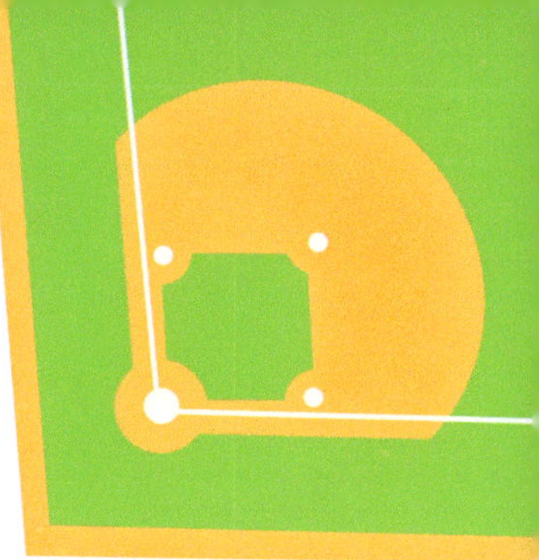

The Boise Hawks are a Minor League Baseball team based in Boise, Idaho's capital city. They play their home games at Memorial Stadium, a bright and lively ballpark known for its fun family atmosphere and beautiful views of the foothills. The Hawks are part of the Pioneer League, and many young players spend time on this team as they build their skills and work toward their baseball dreams.

FOOTBALL

The Boise State Broncos are one of Idaho's most popular football teams, and families all across the state cheer for them every season. The team plays its home games at Albertsons Stadium in Boise, a loud and energetic place best known for its bright blue turf, which fans lovingly call "The Blue." The Broncos are part of college football's Mountain West Conference and are known for their exciting plays and strong team spirit.

The western white pine is Idaho's state tree. It's known for its tall, straight trunk and soft, flexible needles that grow in bundles of five. The western white pine was officially adopted as the state tree in 1935, and its towering height and gentle beauty have made it a proud symbol of Idaho's forests and mountain landscapes.

The cutthroat trout is Idaho's state fish. It's a colorful freshwater fish known for the bright red or orange streaks under its jaw that make it easy to recognize in clear rivers and mountain streams. The cutthroat trout was officially adopted as the state fish in 1990.

Can you name these?

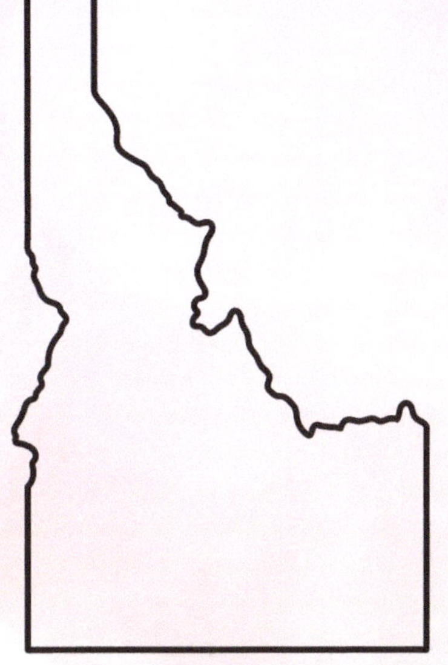

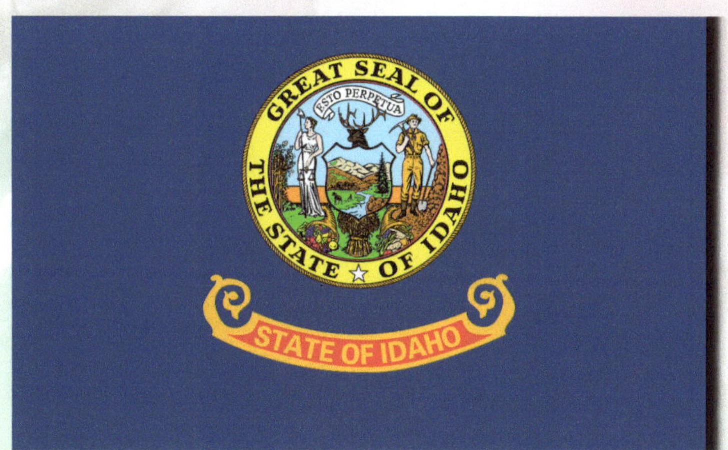

I hope you enjoyed learning about Idaho.

To explore fun facts about the other 49 states, visit my website at www.joeysavestheday.com. You'll also find a wide variety of homeschool resources to support joyful learning at home. If you enjoyed this book, I would be grateful if you left a review. Your feedback truly helps. Thank you for your support!

Check out these other interesting books in the 50 States Fact Books Series!

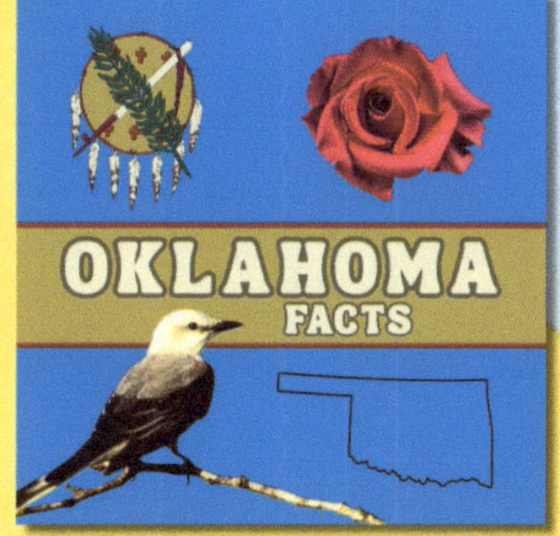

www.mimibooks.com

www.ingramcontent.com/pod-product-compliance
Lightning Source LLC
LaVergne TN
LVHW070200110826
845147LV00002B/452

* 9 7 8 1 9 5 8 9 8 5 9 4 6 *